Kids' View of the World

Candice Dunn & Rebecca Mann

MURDOCH BOOKS

xOx

God is a man who makes love, marriage is a lucky dip. Babies are made from Daddy's eggcracker, and you'll go to hell if you pick your nose.

This is our wonderful world from the viewpoint of Australian kids between the ages of four and 13. We asked these kids some tough questions about where we come from, growing up, love and marriage, and where we go when we die. They shared with us their insightful, innocent and sometimes funny views.

We know
all about the world,
where we came from +
how we got here

It all started with tiny germs that stuck together. Elizabeth (10)

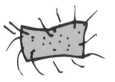

God made cavemen first. Didn't like them. So he
started again and made people. Katie (10)

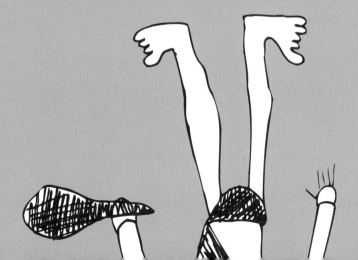

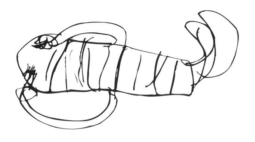

Babies start off as little worms that grow heads and arms and legs which turn them into babies. James (6)

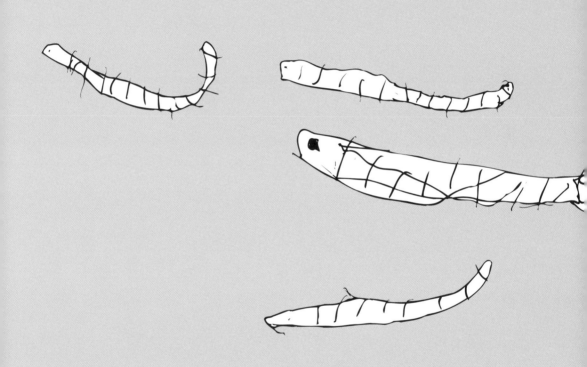

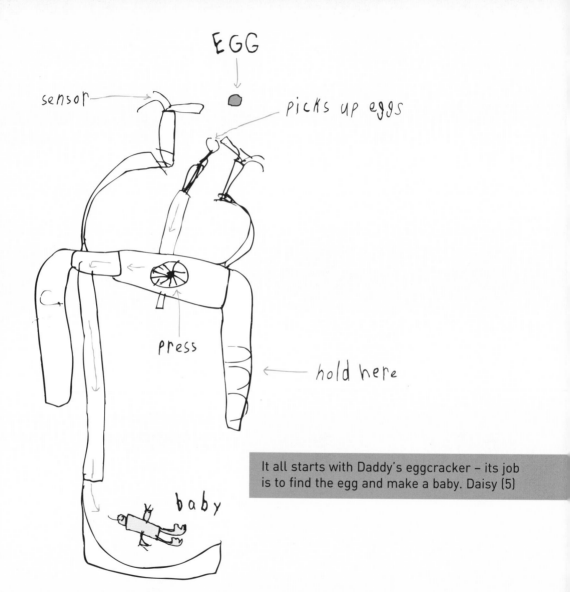

EGG

sensor

picks up eggs

press

hold here

baby

It all starts with Daddy's eggcracker – its job is to find the egg and make a baby. Daisy (5)

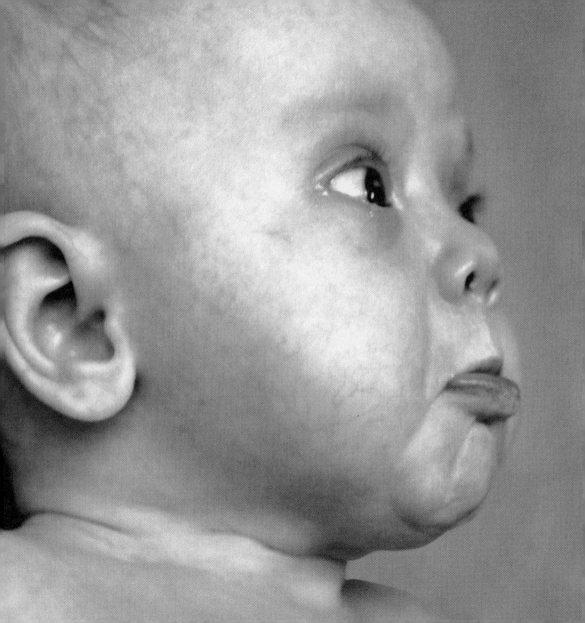

Before I was born I used to be a monkey. India (5)

Not to mention growing up

I can't wait to grow up so I can do dangerous things like cooking. Grace (5)

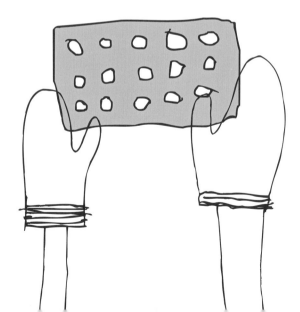

Growing up is not much fun 'cause you won't get to go to theme parks. Harrison (9)

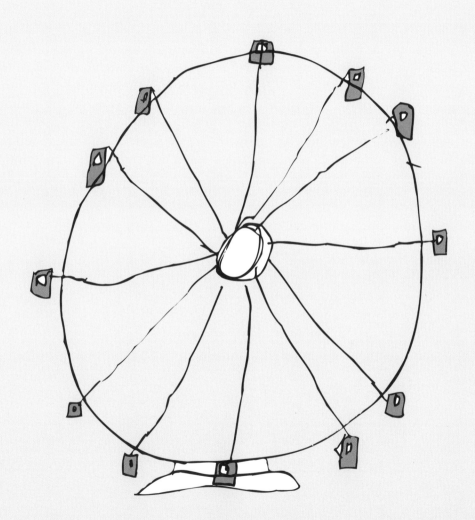

When I grow up I want to be famous – then you'll get a lot of attention and slaves who do everything for you. Amelia (8)

Growing up scares me because all the girls are going to want to kiss me. Sage (5)

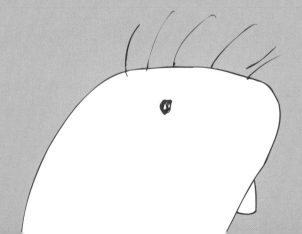

We've already worked out the secrets of love

I don't mind the idea of love but the only boy I love is my Daddy. Nicky (5)

I can tell when one of my friends is in love 'cause they look odd. Poppy (5)

You have to be 20 years or older for dating 'cause young people can't find a girlfriend that quickly. Thomas (9)

I guess I'll start dating in my teens. It's sort of when you're old but not too old – still small but not too small. Zoe (8)

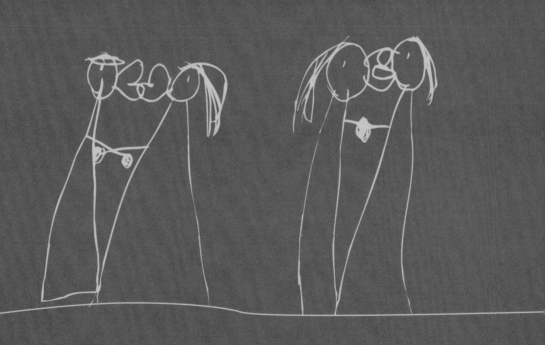

...And the truth about marriage

Marriage is like a lucky dip. You never know what ring you're going to get. Jack (9)

People get married so they can get some money to buy a house and a car. Myles (7)

It looks silly if you get married when you're a kid 'cause everyone will just think you're the flower girl. Jessie (6)

I don't think I'll be getting married and having kids.
A wife and kids will just bug me. Jaspar (9)

And we know what it takes
to be a good
Mum + Dad

A Dad's job is to embarrass his kids. Natasha (10)

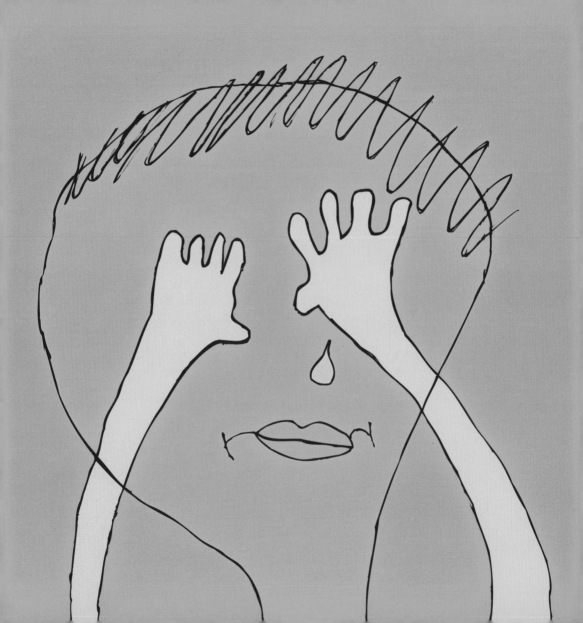

Mums do cooking for us after a hard day. Sam (5)

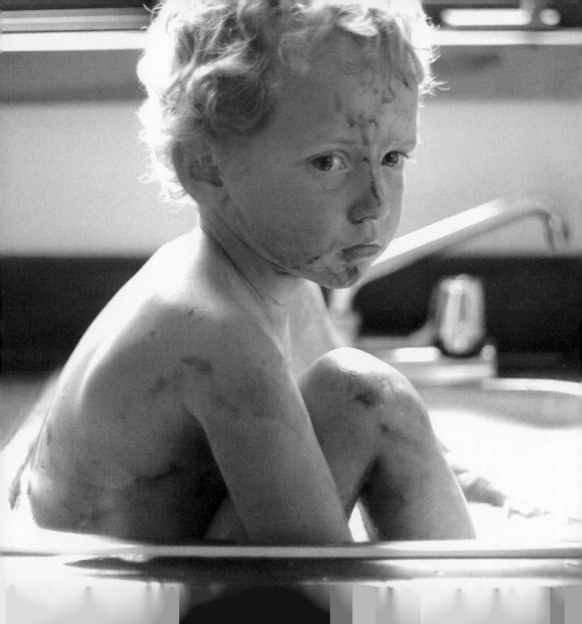

If I didn't have a mum I wouldn't know how
to cook and turn on the bath. Daniel (7)

Dads just eat junk and are always at work. Brooke (6)

We even know what happens when you die

The rule is when you die, you have to stay in the graveyard for two years before you can go to heaven. Spencer (7)

You go to hell if you do bad things like kill someone,
rob someone or pick your nose. Ellie (11)

Our fish jumped out of the tank and dried up in the fruit bowl. I see him in the clouds now. Tom (6)

we know about God and His friends

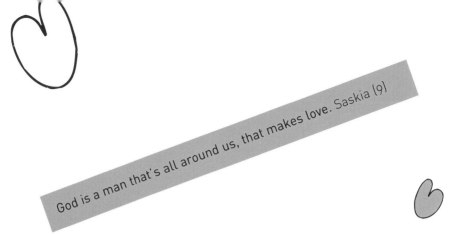

God is a man that's all around us, that makes love. Saskia (9)

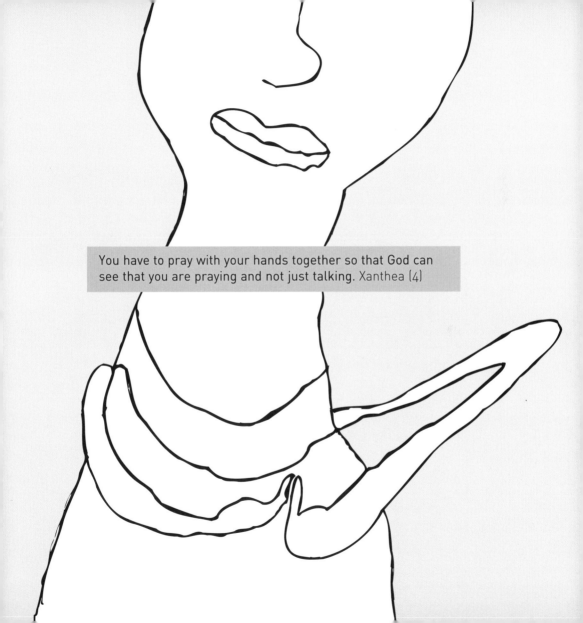

You have to pray with your hands together so that God can see that you are praying and not just talking. Xanthea (4)

The first person that died on earth was Baby Jesus.
He was 50 years old. Johnnie (5)

Mary looks down on you when you pray. If God can't see you, she says, 'Look, there's someone praying for you.' Lucy (9)

We also believe things
you don't

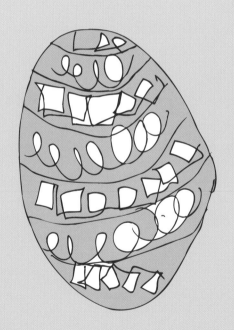

Easter is when your parents lay eggs in the garden. Gabrielle (8)

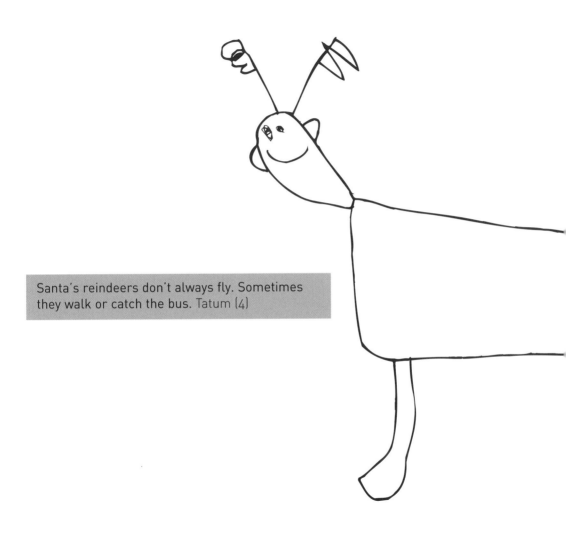

Santa's reindeers don't always fly. Sometimes they walk or catch the bus. Tatum (4)

Angels are things that come get your teeth at night. Sebastian (6)

Fairies can't sleep because their wings never stop flying. Emily (4)

We know how to make
the world
a better place

Not to litter, don't start fires and don't start wars. Jake (8)

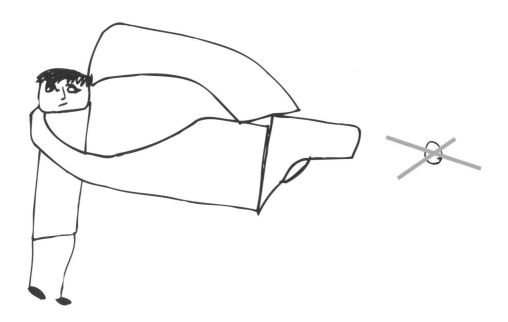

I'd stop the army from going to war. They can do garbage duty instead. Paul (5)

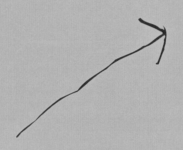

To stop wars, I'd send each person to their bedroom. Hannah (4)

But
the most important thing
to remember about the
world is...

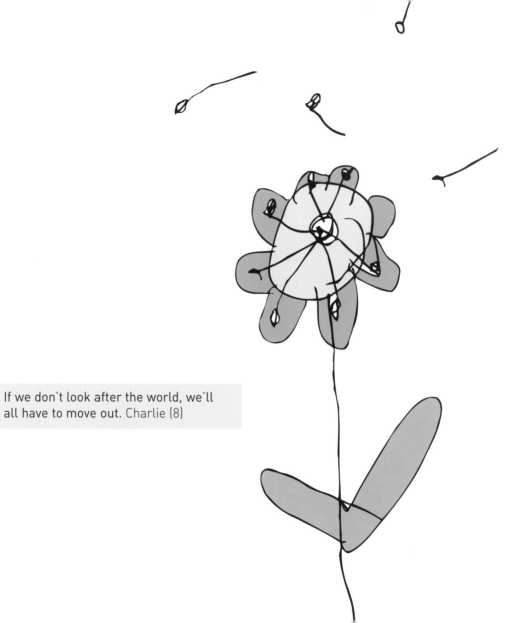

If we don't look after the world, we'll all have to move out. Charlie (8)

ACKNOWLEDGMENTS

Thank you to all the gorgeous children we have had the pleasure of meeting and for allowing us to share in their worlds. Also, to all the mums and dads who willingly let us interrogate their children for hours on end. And special thanks go to the little creative geniuses who happily provided the wonderful drawings that feature in this book: Finn (5), Gigi (7), Indi (7), Jonas (7), Lewis (7), Liv (7), Speedo (7), Spencer (6) and Tatum (4).

Visit www.kidsviewoftheworld.com to find out more about what kids think and to share your kids' stories and quotes.

Published in 2006 by Murdoch Books Pty Limited.

Murdoch Books Australia
Pier 8/9, 23 Hickson Road
Millers Point NSW 2000
Phone: + 61 (0) 2 8220 2000
Fax: + 61 (0) 2 8220 2558
www.murdochbooks.com.au

Murdoch Books UK Ltd
Erico House, 6th Floor North
93–99 Upper Richmond Road
Putney, London, SW15 2TG
Phone: + 44 (0) 20 8785 5995
Fax: + 44 (0) 20 8785 5985

Chief Executive: Juliet Rogers
Publisher: Kay Scarlett

Design Manager: Vivien Valk
Designer: Vanessa Block
Editor: Siobhán Cantrill
Production: Maiya Levitch

Picture credits: cover and internal images by Getty Images, except pages: 14, 51 (Fotosforme); 87 (Stockbyte); and 95 (Corbis).

National Library of Australia
Cataloguing-in-Publication data:

Dunn, Candice.
Kids' view of the world : big thoughts from little people.

ISBN 1 74045 863 X
ISBN 978 1 74045 863 4

1. Children - Australia - Quotations.
2. Conduct of life - Quotations, maxims, etc.
I. Mann, Rebecca. II. Title.

808.882

Printed in China by Midas Printing (Asia) Ltd in 2006.
Reprinted 2006 (twice), 2007.